The Great Welsh Women Colouring Book

Written & Illustrated by Diana Matos Gagic

**First published in 2021 by
Crafty Birdie Designs**

Text copyright © Diana Gagic, 2021
Illustrations copyright © Diana Gagic, 2021

Design for print by
Emma Gregg

Edited / proofread by
Emma Turner
Ian Park

Created in Yorkshire

The moral right of Diana Gagic to be identified as the author and illustrator
of this work has been asserted in accordance with Sections 77 and 78
of the Copyright, Designs and Patents Act 1988.

All rights reserved.
No part of this book may be reproduced, transmitted or stored in any form
or by any means, graphic, electronic or mechanical, including photocopying, taping
and recording, without prior written permission from the publisher.

Email: craftybirdies@gmail.com
Etsy: CraftyBirdieDesigns

Printed in England

ISBN 978-1-9160072-5-3

This book has been made with responsibly sourced uncoated paper (and love) and is suitable for colouring in using pens, pencils or crayons of your choosing... so feel free to be as creative as you like!

About the Author / Illustrator

Diana has lived for many years in the beautiful, historic Yorkshire village of Haworth, home to the famous Brontë family during the Victorian era. Like the Brontës, Diana loved to draw and create as a young girl and remains passionate about the arts, nature, truth and equality. This hand-illustrated book evolved from a desire to help keep alive the memory of some great, inspirational women; aiming to honour brave ladies who battled the odds to stand up for what they believed in and in doing so helped to encourage new generations to aim for their dreams and be true to themselves.

Welsh Women

Our history books are disproportionately filled with the great achievements of men. Probably not helped by the fact that until the 19th century, a woman's property – including intellectual property – automatically became her husband's when married! Female contributions to society were often overlooked. This book aims to highlight and celebrate some remarkable Welsh women, pioneers from the past and present, whose works have helped to transform the lives of others, and in many cases, the course of history. Just a little token of remembrance for great women everywhere.

Sarah Jane Rees
(1839 - 1916)

Born in rural Ceredigion near Llangrannog, Sarah Jane was better known by her bardic name of Cranogwen. She succeeded in her determination to live a less conventional life by becoming a pioneer in many fields — mariner, poet, teacher, editor and social reform campaigner. The strong-willed daughter of a mariner, she insisted that she accompany her father to sea, rejected a career as a dressmaker and demanded an education when it was unusual for girls to receive one. She gained a master's certificate which qualified her to captain a ship in any part of the world and set up her own navigation school, with herself as head-teacher, at just 21! In 1865 her remarkable writing skills turned her into a Welsh celebrity when she became the first woman to win a poetry prize at the National Eisteddfod. Her winning poem 'Y Fodrwy Briodasol' – The Wedding Ring – was a moving satire on the married woman's destiny. A successful collection of her poems was published in 1870 and she went on to become the first female editor of a women's magazine in Wales in 1879, allowing her a platform to further advocate the education of women. She defied stuffy Victorian society by openly leading a lesbian lifestyle. In 1901, concerned with the welfare of women and children in dysfunctional families, she founded the South Wales Women's Temperance Union promoting an alcohol-free way of life.

Frances Hoggan
(1843 - 1927)

Frances Hoggan was born in Brecon in Powys and became the first female doctor to be registered in Wales. She was also the first British woman to receive a doctorate in medicine from any European university. Due to the exclusion of women from taking professional examinations in the UK at the time, she resourcefully obtained her medical doctorate from the University of Zurich in 1870, completing the six-year course in just three years! As a pioneering medical practitioner, researcher and social reformer, she played a significant role in the battle for British women to be allowed to study medicine in the nineteenth century — The British Medical Association finally accepted female doctors in 1892. She became a specialist in women's and children's diseases and helped to establish a system of secondary schools for girls in Wales. She later became involved in education and social reforms in South Africa, the Middle East, India and the US. The Learned Society of Wales presents the annual Frances Hoggan Medal to recognise the contribution of outstanding women in science, technology, engineering, medicine or mathematics.

Elizabeth Andrews
(1882 - 1960)

Elizabeth was one of 11 children born into a poor mining family at Hirwaun in the Cynon Valley and at just 13 she was obliged to leave school in order to help her parents make ends meet. Enduring adversity inspired her to become the first female organiser of the Labour Party in Wales. A true champion of women's and children's rights, she became known as 'Our Elizabeth' to the women she helped. She joined the women's suffrage movement and was one of three women who gave evidence before the House of Lords to highlight the poor housing conditions and high death rates among the children of working-class mining families. Elizabeth's campaign made an impact and pit head baths were made compulsory in 1924, improving sanitation and overall family health in the homes of the workers. Her motto was "Educate, Agitate, Organise." In these pre-NHS times Elizabeth worked tirelessly to improve maternity and childcare, establishing a service of clinics, midwives, home helps and one of the earliest nursery schools in Wales. She was also one of Britain's first female magistrates and was awarded an OBE in 1948 for her contribution to public services.

Margaret Haig Thomas
(1883 - 1958)

Margaret Haig Thomas was born into an extremely comfortable life but she used her privilege as 2nd Viscountess Rhondda in a selflessly noble way — to fight for the rights of all women. Lady Rhondda was a successful businesswoman and the first female to be President of the UK Institute of Directors. She was the creator and editor of an influential magazine, a civil servant and a leading suffragette. She famously spearheaded the suffrage campaign among the women of South Wales and grabbed the attention of the anti-suffrage Prime Minister Asquith by jumping on his car! As a militant member of the Women's Social & Political Union (WSPU) she was briefly imprisoned and endured a hunger strike for the cause. During the First World War she survived the sinking of the Lusitania, then went on to be the Commissioner for the Women's National Service Department in Wales, responsible for recruiting female workers. In 1921 she founded The Six Point Group feminist campaign for fairer laws on political, occupational, moral, social, economic and legal rights.

Elaine Morgan
(1920 - 2013)

Born into a poor mining family in Hopkinstown, near Pontypridd, Elaine won a writing scholarship to Oxford University and went on to become a pioneering TV writer, author, evolutionary theorist and feminist icon. Married with three children, her writing breakthrough began in the 1950s after winning a competition in the New Statesman magazine. The BBC produced her scripts for television, making her one of the first women to make an impact in the male-dominated world of the small screen at this time. In a career spanning 30 years she won many awards and wrote some of the best-loved dramas in television history. She is the author of several successful books which concentrate on social science and human evolution. Her first book, The Descent of Woman, published in 1972, became an international bestseller and was an important text in the Women's Liberation movement at that time. She was appointed OBE in 2009 and in the same year was elected a Fellow of the Royal Society of Literature.

Laura Ashley
(1925 - 1985)

Born in Dowlais, Merthyr Tydfil, Laura grew up to become a world-renowned fashion designer and the name behind a global textiles business empire. Initially inspired by a Women's Institute exhibition on traditional handicrafts at the V&A Museum, Laura and her husband Bernard, unable to find suitable fabrics in the shops, taught themselves fabric printing from library books to create the designs she wanted! From these humble beginnings in rural mid-Wales in 1953, the enterprising couple brought employment and opportunity to a deprived area and their business developed into an internationally successful ladies fashion and home furnishings brand representing the best in British design. Due to its incredible turnover and growth, a Queen's Award for Export was given to the Laura Ashley company in 1977. The family business established the Laura Ashley Foundation in 1987, with a focus on supporting the arts, and this charity legacy evolved into The Ashley Family Foundation in 2011 with the aim of supporting a broad range of rural community arts and social welfare projects.

Mary Quant
(b.1930)

Dame Barbara Mary Quant is a design and retail pioneer of Welsh heritage who became the most iconic fashion designer and trend setter of the 'Swinging Sixties' scene. Following her parents' refusal to let her attend a fashion course, Quant had studied illustration at Goldsmiths before starting out as a self-taught designer. She attended evening classes on cutting and adjusting mass-market printed patterns to achieve the innovative looks she was after. Commonly credited with inventing the decade's most iconic look – the mini-skirt – Quant's designs epitomized the 'London Look' which provided a fresh departure from the structured mainstream clothing at the time. Quant wanted bold and practical outfits which allowed freedom of movement – "relaxed clothes suited to the actions of normal life." In 1966 she was appointed Officer of the Order of the British Empire (OBE) for her outstanding contribution to the fashion industry and in 1990 she won the Hall of Fame Award of the British Fashion Council. She was appointed Dame Commander of the Order of the British Empire (DBE) in 2015 for services to British fashion.

Betty Campbell
(1934 - 2017)

Betty Campbell was born into a poor household in Butetown and went on to become immortalised as the first statue of a named, real woman in the whole of Wales! She was Wales' first black headteacher in the 1970s and an inspirational community activist who championed multi-cultural education. Inspired by a trip to the US where she learned about anti-slavery abolitionists like Harriet Tubman and the civil rights movement, she said: "I was determined that I was going to become one of those people and enhance the black spirit, black culture as much as I could." The children in her school were taught about slavery, black history and the system of apartheid which operated at the time in South Africa. Campbell served as a councillor on Cardiff City Council and helped to create Black History Month in the UK. She was a board member of BBC Wales in the 1980s, was made an honorary fellow of Cardiff Metropolitan University and, in 2003, she was awarded an MBE for services to education and community life.

Shirley Bassey
(b. 1937)

Dame Shirley Bassey, DBE, was born in Tiger Bay, a poor multi-cultural area of Cardiff. Her father was Nigerian and her mother came from Teesside. As a child, her teachers noticed Bassey's strong voice but gave her little encouragement: "...everyone told me to shut up. Even in the school choir the teacher kept telling me to back off till I was singing in the corridor!" Bassey's expressive vocal skills were, however, put to good use when she went on to become the first Welsh person to gain a No. 1 single with "As I Love You" in 1959. To date, she has released 70 albums and sold nearly 140 million records, in addition to recording the soundtrack themes to the James Bond films; Goldfinger (1964), Diamonds Are Forever (1971) and Moonraker (1979). This huge success was a remarkable achievement for a girl who left school aged 14 to pack chamber pots! In 2000, Bassey was appointed a Dame for her services to the performing arts and she remains one of the most popular female vocalists in Britain. She headlined Glastonbury music festival in 2007 at the age of 71!

Carol Vorderman
(b. 1960)

Carol Jean Vorderman was brought up in Prestatyn, North Wales, and has become a national treasure as an inspirational mathematician, educational author and television presenter. After gaining a Masters degree in Engineering at the University of Cambridge, Vorderman's breakthrough into television came when her mother noticed a newspaper advertisement asking for "a woman with good mathematical skills" to appear as co-host on a new quiz show. She displayed her brilliant mental arithmetic skills on Countdown from 1982 until 2008. She has gone on to work with Prime Ministers on education and became the first female Honorary Group Captain for the RAF. She is a member of the Royal Institution and has been granted four honorary doctorates and fellowships from different Universities in Britain. Vorderman was honoured as a Member of the Order of the British Empire (MBE) for her services to broadcasting in 2000.

Tanni Grey-Thompson
(b. 1969)

Carys Davina Grey-Thompson, better known by her childhood nickname 'Tanni' was born in Cardiff, Wales. Born with spina bifida, a condition in which a baby's spine and spinal cord does not develop properly in the womb, she went on to become one of the UK's most successful athletes and a global ambassador for disability sport. As a wheelchair racer she won 16 Paralympic medals, including 11 Gold, set over 30 world records and won the London Marathon six times! Following her retirement from the track she became a sports commentator and motivational speaker. For her services to sport she was appointed Member of the Order of the British Empire (MBE) in 1993, advanced to Officer of the Order of the British Empire (OBE) in 2000, and promoted to Dame Commander of the Order of the British Empire (DBE) in 2005. Her BA (Hons) degree in Politics came in handy when, in 2010, Tanni was created a Life Peer in the House of Lords, taking the title Baroness Grey-Thompson of Eaglescliffe. She is the Chancellor of Northumbria University and in 2019 was given the BBC Sports Personality of the Year Lifetime Achievement Award.

Charlotte Church
(b. 1986)

Charlotte Church, born in Llandaff, Cardiff, is a world-renowned singer who rose to fame in childhood for her classical operatic skills and her ability to sing in English, Welsh, Latin, Italian and French! Her talents were spotted in 1997, at just age 11, when she sang Andrew Lloyd Webber's 'Pie Jesu' over the telephone, live on air, on the television show This Morning. As an adult she has experimented with an indie/pop singer-songwriting style and has sold more than 10 million records worldwide overall! Ever versatile, Charlotte has also worked as an actress and hosted her own television show 'The Charlotte Church Show' in the 00s. She is more recently known as a political activist and the founder of an educational charity – The Awen Project – which is a community-focused, free to attend, democratic school. It aims to provide an alternative and progressive way of educating our next generations in a more self-directed way to encourage creative individuality and inner confidence in an ever changing world.

Emily Penn
(b. 1987)

Emily Penn was born in Swansea, South Wales, and went on to become a sailor, artist, research scientist, public speaker and world oceans environmentalist. After graduating from Cambridge University, she joined a globe-circling voyage, where she was shocked to sail through 'The Great Pacific Garbage Patch' in the North Pacific Ocean. This set her on a path of dedicating her life to developing solutions to sea pollution. She organised the largest ever community-led clean-up from a tiny Tongan island and trawled for micro-plastics through the Arctic Northwest Passage. She co-founded eXXpedition in 2014; a series of all-female voyages focused on scientific studies to explore the impact of plastic pollution in global waters and the relationship between waste toxins and female health. She is the youngest, and only, female recipient of both the Yachtsmaster of the Year and Seamaster of the Year awards. Emily was awarded the British Empire Medal in the 2021 Queen's New Year Honours List for services to conservation and to charity.